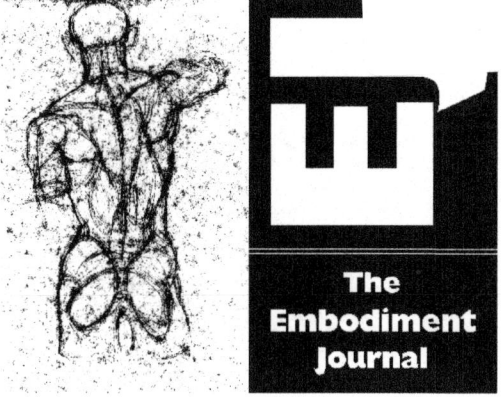

Copyright © Francis Briers 2015

Copyright for the individual articles remains with the authors.

Due reference to original publication in this text to be acknowledged

upon re-publication.

ISBN: 978-0-9567799-6-0

A copy of this book has been deposited with the British Library.

Published by Warriors of Love (WOL) Publishing

www.embodimentjournal.com

The Embodiment Journal

Volume Two

Spring-Summer 2015

Contributors:

Francis Briers is the founder and editor of The Embodiment Journal. He is a Senior Consultant with a boutique leadership consultancy and one of the lead trainers on the Embodied Facilitator Course which is the first European home-grown training for business trainers and coaches to learn to work with the body and for 'body people' to learn how to work in business. Francis has been exploring the mind-body connection for 20 years and his studies include a 3rd Dan black belt in Kodo Ryu Karate, being a certified Uzazu embodiment coach, and a degree from one of the UK's top drama schools. He has developed his own approach to embodiment working in detail with posture called 'Somatic Presence.'

Find out more about the Embodied Facilitator Course at: www.embodiedfacilitator.com

Diane Parker is a former dancer who now works independently as a creative coach and dance movement psychotherapist. She has worked with a diverse client range in a variety of settings, including special educational needs and forensic psychotherapy, and she currently works in private practice and community mental health. Diane has a specialist interest in working with girls and women around body image, relationships and sexuality, and she is the contributor to a forthcoming volume on dance therapy, trauma and violence drawing on her work with female inpatients of a medium-secure forensic unit, to be published by Jessica Kingsley Press in 2016.

Email: creativecoach@hotmail.com

Pete Hamill MSc, BSc (Hons), CertCoun, Master Somatic Coach (MSC)
Pete Hamill is a consultant, facilitator and coach with an international background in leadership and organisational development. He is also the author of *Embodied Leadership: The Somatic Approach to Developing your Leadership*, published by Kogan Page. Pete runs his own business, Uncommon Leaders Ltd, and his current clients include Barclays, Boston Consulting Group, BP, KPMG and the UK & Singapore Civil Services. Pete has previously worked at Roffey Park Institute for five years, and continues to work as faculty on their MSc in People & Organisational Development, and their Post-Graduate Certificate in Coaching.

Pete completed an intensive four-month training internship with Dr. Richard Strozzi-Heckler at Strozzi Institute in 2003. He has been certified as a Master Somatic Coach and has completed a Certificate in Humanistic Counselling with the Gestalt Centre. He has also completed an MSc in Change Agent Skills & Strategies at the University of Surrey, where his dissertation focused on conflict in teams. In addition Pete is licensed to deliver Barry Oshry's Organisation Workshop and is certified to use the FIRO-B, Change Style Indicator, SDI, and the Global Leadership Profile (GLP) psychometric instruments. Pete lives in Brighton UK, with his wife and young daughter, and loves travel, reading, good food and fine wines!

www.embodiedleadership.net

Deborah Turnbull is excitedly awaiting the first print run of her pamphlet Devotions with Flux Gallery Press, to which she and Tony Flynn have contributed ten poems each. Her work has also appeared in Ink, Sweat & Tears literary webzine. Deborah is putting the finishing touches to Trial by Scar — her first full collection concerning what it takes to thrive amid life's inevitable turbulence. She lives in Brighton with her partner Tom, and children Poppy, Penelope and Brandon, and has worked as a Doula assisting birth and breastfeeding since 2008. She aims to leave land-loving behind and be living on a boat with her family within the year.

www.deborahturnbull.blogspot.co.uk

Mark Walsh is Director of Integration Training Ltd, the Embodied Facilitator Course and Achilles Resilience Training. He is an aikido blackbelt, long term meditator and has trained in numerous embodied systems such as yoga, body therapy, forms of dance and other martial arts.

He has extensive training and facilitation experience, primarily around leadership and resilience/trauma with large and small organisations in the UK and abroad, including: Unilever (London/ Switzerland), The UK House of Lords, Virgin Atlantic, Harrow Primary Care Trust (NHS London), The Institute of Development Studies (University of Sussex, Brighton), Shell, Axa, The Natural History Museum (London), Emerging Capital Partners (US/ Africa), Liberty Global (international telecoms blue-chip) and the Army of Sierra Leone. He also spent three years organising projects, training and conferences for the international organisation Aiki Extensions Inc in areas of conflict. This included leadership training, stress management and conflict resolution work in the Middle East alongside the UN, in the slums of Brazil and with an HIV awareness charity in East Africa.

http://www.integrationtraining.co.uk

Zia Ali is a leadership and conflict resolution trainer, coach and doctoral researcher. He is based in North London and actively involved with mentoring charity A Band of Brothers, in co-facilitating 'rite of passage' mentoring programmes for young male offenders. Zia is also an Interfaith Minister, an artistic performer and creator of the PeaceFire Project, which delivers leadership and peace-building programmes using what Zia calls 'Performance Ritual'.

www.peacefireproject.org

Tom Kenward works as a senior consultant at the Roffey Park Institute. He runs the *MSc in People and Organisation Development* and an Open Programme, *Leading with Presence*. He also designs and delivers bespoke programmes to develop leaders and organisational development practitioners, using somatic methods as part of these. He does his best to practice (and practise) what he preaches with lightness, at work and also with his partner Charlotte and two young children Toby and Rose, sometimes remembering to call forth in the more testing moments the Buddhist mantra of "begin again".

On LinkedIn: http://linkd.in/1DYoD0E

Introduction - Francis Briers

Volume Two! Although it is only the second one out, it still feels like a grand thing to have got even this far. I have been repeatedly struck as I have spoken to people about the Journal and gathered and edited the articles you will read here how wonderfully generous people can be. I see how fully the writers who have authored the articles you will read have given of themselves, how unconditionally they have shared their work. When I look at what they are offering to the world I feel inspired and a little more hopeful.

While I am, of course, looking to ensure there is a complementary range of articles in these pages, I like to give free rein to the contributors as they write. I want them to write about what they are passionate and curious about, what is most alive for them. As such it is a joyful synchronicity to see, as I have curated the work, that there is a kind of flow – almost a theme – through the articles. Pete Hamill elegantly explores how patterns of behaviour are embedded in our soma, Diane Parker shares her story of personal healing and transformation (transforming some of her patterns), Mark Walsh explores his hard-earned wisdom on the links between trauma, conflict, and peace-building, Zia Ali also explores conflict resolution and peacebuilding through ritual and a systemic perspective, and then Tom Kenward expresses his journey with embodiment – especially looking at the benefits of shifting from our 'small' personality to our 'large' centred-self. It seems to me that all of these pieces explore in their own ways the healing of conflict – how we can be conflicted within ourselves, in conflict with each other, and in cycles of conflict in the wider world and across generations. This work is of vital importance in the world today: a world in conflict, too often led by people unwilling to face their internal battles so they can find the courage to do the right things rather than the expedient things.

As such, it is with great pride that I invite you to dive into the pages of Volume Two of The Embodiment Journal.

I hope your life is as enriched by these articles as mine has been.

The purpose of The Embodiment Journal: I wanted to create a place where the leading thinking on embodiment could be shared openly both between practitioners and as an introduction for those newly interested in the field. Like so many things, the field of embodiment has the potential to become a divided community separated by areas of interest, traditions, teachers, and theories of best practice. While I would hope for there to be some common areas, especially in terms of best practice, my intention in founding this journal is to create a "nondenominational" space to share our thinking and collectively evolve the field both in terms of how we do what we do and how widely the gifts of embodiment can be shared for the good of individuals, society, humankind, and indeed the Planet.

You'll see different perspectives and ways of working expressed and described - that is deliberate. There is no single 'right' way of working with the body or practicing embodiment. There are some principles of rigorous and ethical practice but many methods and philosophies. I think that is healthy and seek here to support the diversity not contain or edit it away. I invite you to explore widely and deeply here and elsewhere and shape your own opinions - inspired perhaps by the rich wisdom of others.

An Editor's note: In several of the following articles an embodiment practice 'Centring' (or 'Centering' in the American spelling) is mentioned. There is some description of this which will hopefully describe it in a useful enough manner if you are not already familiar with some kind of centring practice. There are many ways to 'centre' but if you want to know more then experiencing it may be most useful. I have made some audio recordings to talk you through two centring methods, one I developed, and another developed by George Leonard (one of the grandfathers of the Human Potential movement and a very formative player in the world of embodiment) You can find them at:

http://www.fudoshin.org.uk/free-resources/exercises/grounding-and-centring/

Changing, moving, growing, healing: an embodiment journey

- Diane Parker

We never really know what we have until it's gone.

It is 2010, and the new year, and the new decade, begins innocuously enough. I am entering my fortieth year, I have a nascent coaching and consultancy practice working with creative professionals and organisations, and I have managed to stay afloat as a self-employed practitioner for the past two years with a combination of private practice and freelance contracts as a writer/editor. In my spare time, I perform as a member of an improvisation troupe, and I occasionally run sessions with various groups teaching improvisation skills for confidence, communication, personal and leadership development.

I love my work, and though uncertainty is the only constant, I am learning to thrive on the not-knowing, and my curiosity, my energy and my open mind lead me down many avenues I would ordinarily have discounted or dismissed in my former life as a full-time editor employed on a salary. I am learning and growing and it seems the future is bright.

Then, suddenly, at the start of 2010, I become inexplicably ill. It begins with a routine examination that leads to a routine procedure, which leads to complications, and a spell in hospital. That leads to a collapse, a further stay in hospital, more tests, and a blood transfusion. Then an infection, which leads to further complications, more drugs, more tests, more transfusions. All in all, I spend the majority of 2010 in and out of hospital, sitting on plastic chairs in waiting rooms for consultations, examinations and procedures, seeing various professionals who oversee a different part of my body – a haematologist for the blood, a gastroenterologist for the gut and a gynaecologist for my uterus. I feel like a meat machine, made up of different components, misbehaving like unruly children crying out for attention but lacking an authority figure, someone to oversee the entire system. Uncertainty and instability loses its glossy sheen and I become frustrated, angry and eventually depressed. My business suffers, my personal life suffers, and I am too weak and sick to care. I, a former dancer, who always prided myself on my strength, my stamina, my energy, my invincibility, become a shadow of my former self. I, who spent my entire adult life getting comfortable in my own skin, am bewildered by my body's refusal to behave. I take it as a personal attack, an insult, and I hate my body for it. I, who always trusted my instinct and my intuition, can now no longer trust this body I live in. If I cannot trust my body, my centre, my gut, how can I trust my own gut instinct? And if I cannot trust my instinct, how can I trust myself? And if I cannot trust myself, how can I trust the world?

I can't be sure what changed for certain.

All I know is that when I realised I had lost my faith in my body, myself, and my ability to feel safe in the world, I knew I had hit rock bottom, and something had to change. Pushing and fighting wasn't getting me anywhere, so I changed tactic and simply allowed it to be. I shut out all the extraneous noise, the 'helpful advice', and I chose to finally listen to myself, to my body, to the small voice within crying out for attention. I told my body that I was here to listen, and I asked my body what she needed. And in the giving of that silence, that space, something slowly began to heal. I slept when I was tired. I ate when I was hungry and what I was hungry for. I said yes to what I wanted. I said no to what I didn't want. With every decision, I chose to check in with my body first and listen to her response. Gradually, my body and I became integrated, no longer at war with each other. We became a partnership. We acted in each other's best interests. Slowly, very slowly, I learned to trust my body again, and as a result, we began to live in harmony.

The experience of getting sick was a humbling one. It taught me that control was an illusion, and though I may have developed mastery over my body as a dancer, I was certainly not in control of it. My experience of the health care system that year also gave me a deeply embodied experience of integration and holism – that though our modern health care system treats symptoms, diseases and body parts, ill-health affects the whole person. Physical and mental illness cannot be separated – I was affected profoundly on a mental, physical, psychological and spiritual level.

I was also confronted with the fact that, despite my dance training and background, I was not equipped to listen to my body. In fact, most technical dance training, including classical ballet and contemporary dance, requires that one do the exact opposite and *not* listen. We dance students are encouraged to override the body's cries of pain, exhaustion and fatigue. I had learned to ignore my appetite, my capacity for pleasure. My body was my instrument, my tool, my form of artistic expression, but in focusing on what it could *do*, I had never allowed myself to get in touch with how it could *be*. It was only in losing what I believed I had, I was able to truly find myself.

In early 2011, I began to emerge from my year of ill-health and found myself working as an editorial consultant for a dance and music conservatoire. This was an organisation with whom I had a long history, one that began in the late 1990s when I attended a summer school there as a dance graduate and took an introductory course in dance movement therapy. Almost 15 years later, the course was no longer running there, but my association with the conservatoire brought those memories flooding back into my cells, bones and muscles, and I found myself reconnecting with that part of me that had lain dormant. A creative and embodied therapeutic practice that connected the whole self – physical, emotional, psychological and spiritual aspects of self – was precisely what I was looking for. My journey to health and wholeness had brought me to this place and the significance of the timing was not lost on me.

I am of the belief that when we take direct action on a plan, the universe conspires to make it happen. I had a seed of an idea that, once planted and watered, flourished into being. I remember sending the first exploratory email to nearby Goldsmiths University, who were now offering the Masters programme originally run by the Laban Centre, and it was as though a chain of events were set in motion that became unstoppable. I had no idea how I would fund the three-year course, how I would keep a roof over my head, and body, mind and soul together, but within a month, I had been invited for interview and offered a place on the course. What was of particular interest to me was that I felt no anxiety or doubt about this next stage of my journey. Excitement, yes, trepidation, certainly – but I was learning to trust my gut, my intuition again, and on this, it was singing out strongly and clearly an affirmative, joyful YES – yes, this is yours, take it.

I began my dance movement psychotherapy (DMP) training in autumn 2011, and finally emerged as a qualified and registered practitioner in summer 2014. Throughout my training, I kept my private coaching practice small but active, and now, as well as running dedicated DMP groups in the mental health sector, I bring my training to bear on my coaching practice with the individuals I work with. Clients come to me with physical and emotional health issues, issues with confidence and self-esteem, and issues in relating on a professional, personal and intimate level. I have always worked with imagery and metaphor in my practice, but now I also draw my clients' attention to physical sensation, and I am increasingly aware of my own somatic sense as I work, even on the telephone, allowing my clients' words to drop into my body and take shape in there.

Recently I was working with my client Audrey, a woman in her late 30s who was struggling with feelings of scarcity and lack, particularly in relation to her personal relationships. I asked her to describe moments in her life when she has felt the opposite of scarcity, ie abundant and able to receive and give love freely. As she was describing these moments, I found myself making small undulating movements which increased in depth and intensity as she was speaking. When I asked Audrey to share an image or sensation that arose for her, she described herself as 'the ocean': deep, powerful, all-encompassing, able to go with the 'ebb and flow' of life and love; as she said: 'the ocean doesn't take anything personally – it just *is*.' I invited her – over the phone – to embody that image and breathe with it, so that she could return to this sensation whenever she was feeling small or scarce or wounded by the behaviour or actions of a significant other. She described the sensations in her body of a vast deep ocean ebbing and flowing, and when I asked her what she was left with, she responded: 'I don't need to create a story around someone's silence or lack of response. It's probably nothing to do with me. Ebb and flow is part of life. And in the meantime, I can still be here, flowing for myself.'

Audrey didn't want to carry around this continuous feeling of scarcity and lack; that there was never enough in her life – enough love, enough warmth, enough attention. She knew intellectually the roots of these feelings – and had worked through these extensively in therapy prior to us working together. But she wanted to *feel* differently, to experience what it felt like to have enough, more than enough, and to be able to give freely without resentment. By drawing her attention to her somatic awareness, she was able to drop the feeling of scarcity and have a somatic experience of abundance by embodying her image of the ocean; an image I felt and embodied before she was able to put it into words.

I feel blessed that I was given the opportunity to develop a different relationship to my body through illness, and that I was inspired to bring that enhanced awareness into my work with others. Sometimes we have to lose ourselves in order to find ourselves again. This is the story of my embodiment journey so far, but the journey is by no means over. If there is one thing I have learned, it is the human body's capacity to constantly make and remake itself and as we *are* our bodies, we also have the capacity to change, grow, develop and transform – emotionally, spiritually and psychologically.

Diane Parker is a former dancer who now works independently as a creative coach and dance movement psychotherapist. She has worked with a diverse client range in a variety of settings, including special educational needs and forensic psychotherapy, and she currently works in private practice and community mental health. Diane has a specialist interest in working with girls and women around body image, relationships and sexuality, and she is the contributor to a forthcoming volume on dance therapy, trauma and violence drawing on her work with female inpatients of a medium-secure forensic unit, to be published by Jessica Kingsley Press in 2016.

Email: creativecoach@hotmail.com

Further reading

Bertherat, T. And Bernstein, C. (1989). The body has its reasons: self-awareness through conscious movement. Healing Arts Press, Vermont.

Halprin, A. (2000). Dance as a healing art: returning to health through movement and imagery. Life Rhythm Books, US.

Shaw, R. (2003). The embodied psychotherapist: the therapist's body story. Routledge, London.

Somatic Marker Theory as a framework for embodiment - Pete Hamill

Think about your most embarrassing moment – ok, maybe not the *most* embarrassing moment, but something that impacted you. Take a moment and really get that back into your mind.

What you'll probably notice is that remembering this moment doesn't just bring back a cognitive, rational memory as purely thought, but you feel a version of what you felt at that time. Perhaps you wanted the ground to open up and swallow you whole, or wished you could be invisible! The memory is stored with something akin to an emotional soundtrack that you re-experience on recall.

These emotional soundtracks are what neuroscientist, Antonio Damasio (2006), refers to as somatic markers. So why do we store emotional soundtracks in this way? Basically they are a means by which evolution has equipped us to deal efficiently with different situations.

Imagine yourself in a complex social situation (meetings, networking events, some family gatherings, school reunions, etc). You don't have time to analyse everyone, their relationships with you, with each other, the political dimensions if this is a work or organisation context, etc. Your neo-cortex doesn't have time to do all of that cognitive work, so the sub-cortical regions of the brain activate somatic markers corresponding to similar historical situations and we experience the appropriate emotional soundtrack.

So, if it's a situation which could be embarrassing the soundtrack of your embarrassing moments will play and you will react by taking action to attempt to ensure that you are not embarrassed. This simple and elegant solution evolved for our safety walking in tribes on the savannahs, not for dealing with today's complex social situations.

But before we get into the unintended consequences of this process, it's important to understand that it is not conscious. (We use conscious processes when we analyse a situation in depth with our neo-cortex). Instead it originates in the older regions of the brain, such as the brain-stem, amygdala and hypothalamus. It communicates directly with our bodies where it generates the feelings that we experience. This is a pre-conscious process, which gets our attention through our feelings, rather than through our thoughts.

So what happens when we experience these feelings? Basically, we react to discomfort by making ourselves more comfortable, just like when you scratch an itch or put on a sweater when you're cold. And, it gets more interesting! Have you ever realised that you had an itch when you're already scratching it? This is reasonably common – we often react to make ourselves more comfortable without being aware we possessed the discomfort.

The same applies with somatic markers. We react to the emotional soundtrack that's playing and we make ourselves comfortable, often without being aware that we were experiencing discomfort.

When we then ask people why they did something, they with either respond with an honest response – "it just felt like the right thing to do," – or they post-rationalise a reason as to why.

Psychologists have been telling us for a long time that humans post-rationalise much (or perhaps even all) of their behaviour. Through

Damasio's work on understanding somatic markers we can now see the mechanism for this.

So how much control do these somatic markers have over our behaviour? This is an interesting question to consider. My argument is that our personality is basically a series of somatic markers that have a strong hold over us. Let's take the following example[1].

Imagine a young child coming out of nursery / kindergarten, moving towards his mother, the object of love and safety. In the next garden there's an old, grumpy dog, that the teachers / carers have warned the children to stay away from, as it might bite them. For this child, this has produced a fear of the dog.

As the child runs towards his mother, the dog starts barking. The mother has come from work and, with multiple concerns in her head, doesn't even hear the dog. The child does, and starts to cry. The mother picks him up and comforts him, trying to find out what is

---

[1] This example is a version of one given by Richard Strozzi-Heckler (Strozzi-Heckler, 1997: 19-29).

wrong. The child can't express what is wrong, and the dog keeps barking so the child keeps crying.

This goes on for some time and eventually the mother, reaching some level of exasperation with an upset she sees no reason for, says: "If you don't stop crying, I'll put you down." The child keeps crying, and eventually the mother puts him down. In this moment the child is separated from safety in what he perceives as a moment of danger, so he learns at a deep level that he made the wrong move. He wants to reconnect with his mother, so what does he do? To stop crying, he tightens his diaphragm, brings the breathing into his upper chest, tightens the jaw, throat and eyes, which stops the expression of the emotion, and, as I will explore later, the feeling of the emotion (by changing the musculature). Now his chin will wobble a little, and he may quietly sob, but the big emotional outburst is contained.

The mother then picks up the child, consoles him again, reinforcing the message that crying was wrong, and that holding in the emotion was correct. (This is by no means an attack on mothers by the way – this is just to illustrate a point.)

This is the process of creating a somatic marker. This person will now begin to feel uncomfortable around emotional upsets – their own or others – and will respond to this discomfort in the same way, by holding in or containing emotion.

If the message to contain emotions is repeated on an ongoing basis, or happens at a particularly significant (or traumatic) moment, then 40 years later you have the man who hasn't cried in 40 years. Over time this just becomes who he is – an aspect of his personality.

This man will have a long term pattern of tightening the diaphragm, shallow breathing, holding the jaw tightly, and tightening the eyes, all of which are required to not feel and express that pattern of emotions. In this way a somatic marker moves from an emotional memory to the shape we take in the world. This is the shape that the person will develop. It is how he will hold himself initially when he feels emotion, but eventually with practice this will just become a normal way of being.

If this man then becomes a manager making others redundant, then he will be uncomfortable seeing the emotion others will experience.

He cannot be comfortable with his own emotions, and when he is called upon to empathise with another's, he will be unable to. Empathy in this situation requires him to feel the emotion he has spent a lifetime restraining. He may then be accused of being brutal or unfeeling in the process.

All aspects of our personality can be understood in the same way. How to behave, what gets rewarded by parents and significant adults, what gets rewarded in childhood social groups, etc. All of these combine to give us our way of operating in the world – an habitual pattern of thoughts, feelings and behaviours which we call our personality.

Notice also that, as illustrated above, this personality is embodied. The personality above can be described in conversation as a repression of emotions, but it is also a shape which is created through tension in the muscles. As Nietzsche (2012: 314) said:

"Our most sacred convictions, the unchanging elements of our supreme values, are judgements of our muscles."

Our culture is also passed on this way. We learn at a young age what is appropriate and inappropriate, but if asked to describe our culture we would have difficulty. The somatic markers aren't a set of rules we learnt in our rational neo-cortex (the most recent part of our brain in evolutionary terms, which allows us to deal with abstract concepts, theories and models); they are more deeply held in our bodies. Therefore, we will generally act in line with our culture, because not to do so just feels wrong. In her book *Watching the English*, (Fox, 2004) cultural anthropologist Kate Fox, who is English herself, describes her experience in breaking the rules of English culture by queue jumping, a most unapproved of behaviour in England. She states:

"Just the thought of queue-jumping was so horribly embarrassing that I very nearly abandoned the whole project rather than subject myself to such an ordeal. I just couldn't bring myself to do it. I hesitated and agonized and procrastinated, and even when I thought I had managed to steel myself, I would lose my nerve at the last minute and slink humbly to the back of the queue, hoping that no one noticed that I had even been considering jumping it." (Fox, 2004: 154-155)

She had to prepare herself for the experience by having a couple of drinks, because it feels such an unnatural and difficult thing to do – the drinks anaesthetize her to her learned somatic markers. This shows the power of somatic markers in guiding our behaviour: we can want to do something, know that we should do it, and be lost in hesitating, agonizing and procrastinating, such that we are unable to do it.

Free Will

I am aware in what I have written so far, that it could appear deterministic –that our behaviours are governed by conditioned responses to somatic markers formed in childhood. And indeed, there are neuroscientists and some psychologists working to prove that there is no free will. They would argue that it appears that we have free will because we believe our post-rationalisations. If we accept them as post-rationalisations then free will disappears, and with it many challenging problems in philosophy, consciousness studies, psychology and neuroscience. It is a viewpoint which is not without its own problems however, which I will not seek to address in detail here. What I would say is that accepting such an argument has disturbing consequences for our ideas of personal responsibility, justice and leadership.

My own view is that for us as human beings, acting from our somatic markers is probable, but not inevitable, and that free will is possible. However it is a possibility that requires something from us.

We need to be able to slow down and see our somatic markers, and the actions that they drive us towards, as they occur within us. This means that we also need to learn to be with our discomforts without trying to fix them or change them; to be comfortable with being uncomfortable.

For many of us this is tough. When we are in a meeting or a social situation and someone says something which in some way diminishes our dignity, we feel it, but often don't fully realise what has happened until later. We then think of all the things we could, or would, or should have said in that moment. Of course, it's too late.

Instead, we feel the discomfort in that moment, and pre-consciously respond with whatever our more normal reaction is – withdrawing, arguing, getting grumpy or passive aggressive – whatever that may be.

Cultivating free will requires us to feel our discomfort fully – facing it, and the somatic marker that lives inside of us. Sitting with our discomfort we can become aware of two things – one, that no discomfort is forever, (that this too shall pass, all on it's own without me having to do anything); and two that we have choice about our responses to discomfort. This is something no one can be told – we must each learn the reality of it for ourselves, through our paying attention to our somatic markers.

In that moment we can choose something other than the reactions we have developed over time to avoid and hide from our discomfort. To use the earlier example, the manager can choose a different response in dealing with emotional upsets – e.g. to relax and be with the other person in their upset, rather than tensing up with his discomfort. It will not be easy, but in sitting with his discomfort rather than reacting to it, he has this choice.

Mindfulness practices which pay attention to sensation in the body (perhaps they should be called bodyfulness practices) can be extremely valuable in the cultivation of our ability to exercise free will.

Cultivation of embodied responses

It is also possible, and necessary to cultivate helpful embodied responses. I described earlier the response to a somatic marker as a pre-conscious process, which gets our attention through our feelings, rather than through our thoughts. The fire fighter, who, on gut instinct, gets his team out of a burning building just before it collapses, is also responding to a somatic marker. This is how these markers can be helpful to us when we pay attention to them.

The psychologist Daniel Kahneman, who won a Nobel Prize in Economics along with Amos Tversky for their groundbreaking work on behavioural economics, addresses some of these questions (Kahneman, 2011). He defines a System 1 and System 2 in our thinking processes. System 1 is the automatic processes that are driven through the body – in the words we have used here, our somatic markers. System 2 is the conscious thought processes that we engage through effort and attention – in the words we have used here, a reasoning process. Kahneman states:

The defining feature of System 2… is that its operations are effortful, and one of its main characteristics is laziness, a reluctance to invest more effort than is strictly necessary. As a consequence, the thoughts and actions that System 2 believes it has chosen are often guided by the figure at the centre of the story, System 1. (Kahneman, 2011:31)

Kahneman has also collaborated with another researcher, Gary Klein (1998) who studies decision making through somatic markers – specifically looking at where it works. Kahneman has repeatedly examined where this mode of decision making lets us down in our thinking.

Klein had examples of fire-fighters, who knew instinctively to leave a building seconds before it collapsed, or chess masters who glimpse a chess board mid-way through a game and can produce the response required to win. All of this happens in such a short time that one cannot deliberately and with effort use a process of reasoning to think through all possible options and come up with a reasoned answer – another process is going on to enable these people to know what to do. In fact, in his research Klein discovered that these people did not generate multiple responses to the situation at all; they generated one possible response, which proved to be the correct one.

By comparison Kahneman, in his research, shows how our automatic systems prove to be very poor at understanding statistics and probabilities, and how much of our intuitive judgement gets us into trouble. In these instances we need to use a process of reasoning to get a sensible and useful response, irrespective of the time that might take. So who's right?

What they uncovered was that they are both right. Our more automatic responses can be both invaluable, and also useless, depending on how we have educated and trained them, and on the environment we are operating in.

We may have generated a series of somatic markers through our upbringing, and we can still learn more helpful ones. The process of learning and cultivating new somatic markers is an in-depth process of learning, relying on Ericsson's work on deliberate practice (Ericsson: 1993, 2006, 2007, 2008), which I will not delve into here. Suffice to say, that it is possible to cultivate new embodied responses through this process.

Conclusions

Somatic Marker Theory provides a means by which we can understand the mechanisms of embodiment. In addition by understanding embodiment through neuroscience, we can understand the mechanisms of neuroplasticity and how we can change.

John Coates, an investment banker turned neuroscientist, shows us how embodied practices support us in working with somatic markers. The somatic markers are processed through the older parts of the brain – brain stem, amygdala, hypothalamus etc, known as sub-cortical regions. These regions have many neurons and connections to our neo-cortex, where we can engage in rational thought and planning, but there are much fewer running in the opposite direction (Coates, 2012: 221-222). This is why it's difficult to think our way into a change, or for a model to truly change behaviour, but why these somatic markers can profoundly impact our thinking. He suggests new training programmes and states (p. 236):

"These training regimes will have to be designed in such a way that they access the primitive brain, not just the rational cortex. Since the body profoundly influences sub-cortical regions of the brain, the new training programmes may turn out to involve a lot more physical exercises than they do at present."

I would go further than Coates and say that in the field of leadership development, not including the body is a mistake. By physical exercises he and I are not referring to the gym exercises that you may do for fitness, but rather exercises that allow us to see and experience our somatic markers, how they drive our behaviours and how we can learn to do something different.

Pete Hamill MSc, BSc (Hons), CertCoun, Master Somatic Coach (MSC) is a consultant, facilitator and coach with an international background in leadership and organisational development. He is also the author of *Embodied Leadership: The Somatic Approach to Developing your Leadership*, published by Kogan Page. Pete runs his own business, Uncommon Leaders Ltd, and his current clients include Barclays, Boston Consulting Group, BP, KPMG and the UK & Singapore Civil Services. Pete has previously worked at Roffey Park Institute for five years, and continues to work as faculty on their MSc in People & Organisational Development, and their Post-Graduate Certificate in Coaching.

Pete completed an intensive four-month training internship with Dr. Richard Strozzi-Heckler at Strozzi Institute in 2003. He has been certified as a Master Somatic Coach and has completed a Certificate in Humanistic Counselling with the Gestalt Centre. He has also completed an MSc in Change Agent Skills & Strategies at the University of Surrey, where his dissertation focused on conflict in teams. In addition Pete is licensed to deliver Barry Oshry's Organisation Workshop and is certified to use the FIRO-B, Change Style Indicator, SDI, and the Global Leadership Profile (GLP) psychometric instruments.

Pete lives in Brighton UK, with his wife and young daughter, and loves travel, reading, good food and fine wines!

www.embodiedleadership.net

References

Coates, J. (2012). *The Hour Between Dog and Wolf: Risk-taking, gut feelings and the biology of boom and bust*. London: Fourth Estate.

Damasio, A. (2006). *Descartes' Error*. London: Vintage.

Ericsson, KA, Krampe, RT and Tesch-Romer, C (1993) 'The role of deliberate practice in the acquisition of expert performance', Psychological Review, 100 (3), pp 363–406.

Ericsson, KA (2006) 'The influence of experience and deliberate practice on the development of superior expert performance', in The Cambridge Handbook of Expertise and Expert Performance, ed KA Ericsson, N Charness, RR Hoffman and PJ Feltovich, pp 683–703 Cambridge University Press.

Ericsson, KA, Prietula, MJ and Cokely, ET (2007) 'The making of an expert', Harvard Business Review, July–August, pp 114–21.

Ericsson, KA (2008) 'Deliberate practice and acquisition of expert performance: a general overview', Academic Emergency Medicine, November, 15 (11), pp 989–94.

Fox, K (2004) Watching the English: The hidden rules of English behaviour, Hodder and Stoughton, London.

Kahneman, D (2011) Thinking Fast and Slow, Penguin (Allen Lane), London.

Klein, G (1998) Sources of Power: How people make decisions, MIT Press, Cambridge, MA.

Nietzsche, F, (2012). *Will to Power: Attempt at a Revaluation of All Values*. London: CreateSpace.

Strozzi-Heckler, R. (1997). *The Anatomy of Change: A way to move through life transitions*. Berkley, CA: North Atlantic Books.

Poetry - Deborah Turnbull

First Born

for Poppy

You gave me life:

announced your own

arrival, shaped

my limbs into

conduits about you.

Faithfully kindled

what never was,

drew warmth

through a vacuum.

First born: dawn

of strident love,

insistent limelight,

December sun.

Nine months,

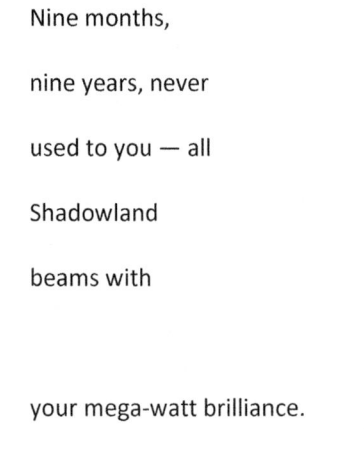

nine years, never

used to you — all

Shadowland

beams with

your mega-watt brilliance.

Retrieval

The bottom is so far down, you delve

darkest waters to your birth. That quiet baby,

the one they *hardly knew they had*,

now skin-to-skin, flutters to life on contact,

erupts in a gladdening cry;

a startled yowl letting air to the lungs.

You resurface through all your years —

babe in adult arms —

shining a new sympathy.

Right, that's it.

I'm making the cut.

Those keratin messengers

of the universe distract.

Going streamline, no more drag.

Five years of growth —

pregnancy, marriage, divorce —

tumbling auburn locks

blunt cut off my face.

Samson's loss is my gain —

head clear of the dead stuff.

The end is just the beginning

sharpened up. Look lively.

Survivor

'If we allow ourselves to experience the death-like sensation of being frozen, and... uncouple the fear ..., we would be able to move through immobility.'
Peter A. Levine — Waking the Tiger, Healing Trauma.

Out of silence comes a rustle, my ears prick.

Pacing in endless vigil for dropped hints

until I can almost see it, track

hair trigger warnings coming closer.

I sleep, never naked, ear to the ground,

and it never comes again. Here in body,

enraptured with memories of gore, the mess,

still faking my own death at an old address.

Out of the woods *primitive* is a dirty word;

we are neat and civil and clever, we are not to flail,

but watch the animals after a wounding —

they shake it out when safe.

Skin spreads in the thaw, colour delivered

to my lips like good news, taking years off me.

The pendulum is back in my hips, tick tock-ing the stride

through each thick moment, knocking the air sideways.

Eyelids flap laquered lashes, create chaos in another country,

and I'm back in the room. Shake that shit out.

Shake it all out — trembling is a gift from the wild.

There is a home here, and it is ours.

Deborah Turnbull is excitedly awaiting the first print run of her pamphlet Devotions with Flux Gallery Press, to which she and Tony Flynn have contributed ten poems each. Her work has also appeared in Ink, Sweat & Tears literary webzine. Deborah is putting the finishing touches to Trial by Scar — her first full collection concerning what it takes to thrive amid life's inevitable turbulence. She lives in Brighton with her partner Tom, and children Poppy, Penelope and Brandon, and has worked as a Doula assisting birth and breastfeeding since 2008. She aims to leave land-loving behind and be living on a boat with her family within the year.

www.deborahturnbull.blogspot.co.uk

The Body of War and Peace - Mark Walsh

Introduction

This article outlines how the causes of war, and trauma caused by war, are embodied, and how peace-building can be done through the body, outlining fundamental concepts and embodied interventions.

Embodiment

Violence remains popular, and to understand its causes and what can be done about it, we need to understand the body. Those committing acts of violence and likewise peace do so through, and with a body. Our way of being, whether it be warlike or peaceful, is embodied or somatic - meaning how we live as bodies not just the common understanding of the body as "brain taxi" (as Francis Briers likes to say). "How we move through space is how we move through life" (Stuart Heller) and if we move in harmonious relationship or not is based on our pattern of awareness, movement, posture etc. The body both expresses and creates 'how we are', including our propensity for war and peace. As a fighter at heart, exposed to violence at a young age, intensive study of the martial arts later and who has worked in areas of conflict on four continents, these matters are not just theoretical to me but passionate engagements. I hope this article is of some use to people involved in embodiment, healing and peace-building which, as we shall see, are one activity.

Trauma and the body overview

The first thing to consider is that war causes trauma, but ALSO, that trauma causes war. "Hurt people hurt people" as Will Bowen said. Trauma is held as a pattern of being, feeling and moving, or usually the lack thereof in the body, as Dr Bessel Van der Kolk's article,'The Body Keeps The Score' [2] expresses. This is now widely accepted even among conventional therapists and trauma has brought embodiment to the wider therapeutic world, as in this domain it simply cannot be ignored. The main symptoms of trauma related conditions such as PTSD involve such things as hyperarousal, numbing (goes alongside freezing), psychosomatic illness, reliving and emotional/relational difficulties through issues with intimacy and self-regulation.[3] These are clearly

---

[2] first published in the *Harvard Review of Psychiatry*, 1994, 1(5), 253-265

[3] 309.81 DSM-IV Criteria for Posttraumatic Stress Disorder

bodily. The list of trauma symptoms is sadly long, so in an article of this size I'll just consider some core aspects and their embodiments:

Hyperarousal

Hyperarousal is a bodily state of stimulation when people are stuck long-term in what is normally a temporary 'fight-flight' level of readiness, with all the psychological and physiological correlates of this such as variation in heart rate, hormone levels and cortical activity. Hyperarousal interferes with listening, makes people more prone to anger (neurologically this is sometimes referred to as an 'amygdala hijack' as blood is diverted from the neocortex to more 'primitive' parts of the brain - if you'll excuse some very crude neuroscience), sleeplessness (too much adrenaline and noradrenaline), anxiety (cortisol levels are up), etc.[4], and crucially for conflict means people are more likely to perceive situations as threatening and respond in anti-social/violent ways. Basically trauma can easily make people rush habitually, make them irritable, uptight,

---

[4] 'Bodily changes in pain, hunger, fear and rage an account of researches into the function of emotional excitement' by Cannon, Walter B, published in 1915

on edge, have difficulties concentrating and make them ready to fight. This happens to individuals (look at how many ex-servicemen are in prison [5] and culturally, as I am struck by every time I work in areas of conflict. As one Afghan elder commented to me, "people are so quick to anger these days over nothing, like they see enemies everywhere" (paraphrased). Happily this hyperarousal can be addressed short-term through state management and long-term through trauma releasing as will be discussed.

Numbing

The other key trauma feature relating to conflict is numbing - when people feel overwhelmed they stop feeling as a protective mechanism. As one of the main ways this happens is through chronic tension (called 'armouring' by body psychologists including Reich) and numbing, lack of movement and therefore awareness go hand in hand. Awareness shrinks, twists (we see this with shame particularly) or becomes out of balance - embodied trauma expert, and founder of the field of embodied peacemaking, Paul Linden calls the former

---

[5] according to the criminal justice campaign group No Offence it's one in ten prisoners – The Independent, Sunday 15 July 2012

"smallifying", as a healthy expansive radiant awareness, and I mean this literally, is lost.

The 'freeze' response is a part of numbing that should also be considered for a richer upstanding of trauma. Freezing - sudden numbing and immobilisation - can lead people to not react when they need to, often leading to guilt if, for instance, someone doesn't fight back during a sexual assault or while on the front lines. A good somatic tool-box therefore includes mobilisation techniques for freezing, as well as relaxation ones for fight-flight.

Interpersonal challenges

Numbing the body leads to negative physical health symptoms of various kinds and effects embodiment on many levels. One of the key ones, combined with hyperarousal, is interpersonal difficulties as our capacity to empathise and connect with others requires that we feel. If I cannot feel myself I cannot feel others, and if I am in a rush and feeling agitated and unsafe I won't want to. Trauma causes disembodiment which makes people literally psychopathic, at least temporarily. This is a strong word but the correct one, and the reason for the seemingly endless cycles of war-trauma-war-repeat in some parts of the world which may be hard to understand by those who have always been safe. Trauma interrupts our ability to find love, safety, trust and belonging on a bodily level. Ironically the felt sense of these very things is healing for trauma, whether it be through an intimate relationship or a therapeutic one that provides these loving conditions. You won't see the word 'love' in many academic papers but understanding the bodily loss of this state and support in re-establishing it is crucial to trauma-recovery and peace building.

Trauma related issues with belonging can cause a shrinking and hardening of one's circles of concern, meaning life becomes 'with us or against us' and 'us vs. them'. This can be seen as a solidification of the 'in' and 'out' groups and has somatic correlates. I have seen this with every traumatised culture I have worked with such as Greeks and Turks, Russians and Ukrainians, Jews and Arabs/ Gentiles, etc. The only exception to this I have observed is with Tibetan refugees who seem almost miraculously inoculated from hate by Buddhist practices and culture. They are frankly impressive in their coping and much can be learnt from them. Mindfulness and Buddhist 'heart practices' such as *metta* meditation which is specially designed for both self-care and to extend ones circle of concern can be key foundations for trauma recovery.

Numbing can also express as boundary issues where people become passive victims unable to say no, over assert boundaries aggressively or do not notice or respect the boundaries of others. Sadly I have seen all of these individually in abused children for example and also culturally in many populations, which may be seen as rude/invasive or overly passive. Trying to understand the Israel-Palestine or Russia-Ukraine conflicts for example, without appreciating this will likely be confusing or frustrating. Embodied work around 'yes' and 'no' is very useful when this is present, as 'boundaries' are not an abstract therapeutic concept, but the way in which a body is predisposed to relate.

NB: While expressed slightly differently – e.g. Russian tense jaws and Israeli movement style (fast, abrupt and linear in Laban[6] movement terms) - limited variations of these somatic patterns exist cross-culturally. They are even in other mammals as you will see in a dog or

---

[6] [Editors Note: If you are not familiar with Laban's work, he studied and taught dance and choreography and developed ways of very specifically classifying movements to the extent that choreography could be recorded in notation like music]

cat that has been mistreated. We have an intuitive sense of them in others which can register as fear, or a sense of someone being 'not right'.

Wider cultural and political considerations

Compounding individual trauma is the general cultural backdrop. With the pace of modern life, disembodying technology use, industrialisation and a general culture of disembodiment in the modern world, it is no wonder trauma is becoming an epidemic even in relatively safe countries. The UK for example has a lifetime prevalence of 80% likelihood of a person experiencing a traumatic incident, so trauma education is relevant to everyone. While violence has always existed and may even be on the decline[7] what is new is a common lack of community, lack of spiritual meaning, disconnection from nature and disembodiment as a general norm, all of which are massive vulnerability factors for acute (short term) trauma responses becoming a longer term condition such as PTSD or GAD and 'normal recovery' - the fact that most people are naturally resilient and recover from trauma - being arrested.

---

[7] Stephen Pinker: The Better Angels of our Nature

Politically we could consider that elites throughout the ages do not want an embodied, untraumatised, feeling population in touch with their own values, as they can be less easily manipulated. Disembodiment is not an accident but a design, a design that benefits the ruling class. Environmentally we could consider that the way we treat ourselves, each other and the planet are the same, and to lose connection to one is to lose connection to all. Disembodiment is a root cause of environmental destruction as well as war, as not feeling is at the root of both. Trauma cuts us off from the 'big body' of the environment as it cuts us off from ourselves and others. I make no apologies for a radically political paragraph in an embodiment journal as I believe that without this wider understanding we will become not only ineffective in our work but complicit in this wider state of affairs.

Centring and state management

The somewhat vague embodiment bucket-term 'centring' refers to various kinds of state management and self-regulation techniques. See for example the ABC centring technique [8] or Wendy Palmer's

---

[8] You can find a video teaching this on Youtube here:

techniques - there are many methods. The principle behind the majority is reducing the fight or flight response through posture, awareness, breathing technique etc, and re-establishing awareness, balance, relaxation, etc (though it's a mistake to think of them as synonymous with this). Centring techniques are extremely important for helping traumatised hyperaroused people learn to manage themselves again, and also for peace building dialogues. As Paul Linden (in my researched opinion THE world leader on centring) said at an Aiki Extensions Inc peace-building event in Cyprus with the UN, attended by aikido teachers from around The Middle East:

"Imagine the person across the negotiating table from you killed a member of your family. You want to talk peace but how do you feel in your body? What do you do?" (Paraphrased).

I have seen peace dialogues and conflict resolution efforts derailed time and time again by bodily fight-flight-freeze response. In fact, I invite readers to think of the last thing they did or said that they regret, almost certainly you were in the FFF response as neurologically it makes us mean and stupid (scientific jargon available on request!). https://www.youtube.com/watch?v=ZwlrQCl0cQk

Words alone are not enough to make peace, we must literally make or shape peace in ourselves first. Happily I have also seen 'centring breaks' used successfully to support constructive conversations, as I did for example in Sierra Leone between factions of the military. I have said much more on centring, how one practices and the necessity for this, how it can be included in yoga or martial arts practice, etc elsewhere. Google/Youtube search if interested in more depth. [Editors note – Mark's Youtube Channel 'Integration Training' has a huge number of high quality videos on embodiment and over 7 million views)

Embodied trauma releasing and other treatments

As well as short-term state management there are various techniques for reducing the chronic embodied trauma symptoms. Many of them use a 'charge' or 'energy' model which I am not a great fan of, but what I do like is that they work. The best known examples are EFT which uses tapping on certain points, David Berchelli's Trauma Releasing Exercises (TRE) which involve facilitating shaking while lying down, both of which can be learnt and self-administered fairly quickly, and EMDR which is an eye movement technique that is National Health Service approved because of its evidence base. I have used all of these personally and rely upon them to stay sane while working somewhere colourful and immediately after, and have found even cynical aid workers open to them if presented in the right way. There is also Hakomi which includes traditional body therapy and mindfulness, and Somatic Experiencing. Both take longer and require years of training to administer but are widely respected. There are also numerous other embodied methods. My current method of choice is Francis Briers' standing trauma releasing form which is similar to TRE in effect but more accessible due to its verticality!

Embodied approaches to building empathy

The primary way we connect is through the body, through touch and coordinated movement specifically. This is why people touch before they talk, why dance is part of courtship worldwide, why soldiers march and why physical activities such as sport are great for building bridges. This understanding can be incorporated into peace building activities in culturally appropriate ways. This can be as simple as encouraging hand shaking or walking side by side (a great coordination or practice) or through the use of explicit techniques such as the classic hand-on-heart listening exercise - YouTube search 'Mark Walsh' and 'listening exercise' to find a video showing this (lower intimacy versions are possible - I have a scale), through taking breaths together to 'sync', to singing etc. The basic principle is getting people to touch, move and breath in sync, in whatever way doesn't freak them out.

Embodied Shadow Work

The most extreme 'othering' that is both a cause and a consequence of conflict, is when aspects of the other (e.g. the Germans, Jews, Arabs or whoever) are actively repressed and denied. This splits the self and means triggering by that group is even more likely and even stronger, and can really get in the way of peace work. When you see an Israeli seemingly overreact and scream in the face of a Palestinian (or vice versa) you are looking at not only the current rational reality of conflict, but the (unhealed) history and also the 'mystery' of disowned self being denied and projected.

Disowned parts of the self can be re-owned through embodied voice dialogue work or simple activities such as moving or standing like that group for a period of time - usually there is an initial discomfort that seems unbearable followed, if a person sticks with it, by an almost disturbing empathy as someone starts to see the world through their enemies' eyes.

Note that this work requires extremely strong group holding and mature therapeutic-level facilitation skills so is not to be taken lightly. It can bring up a lot of painful issues for participants (who must be both willing and well resourced), and there can also be surprising and sudden somaticisation. This is true of any trauma work - do your own work first! - but particularly true of embodied shadow work. In one early experiment with this in the Middle East I became so dizzy I had to sit down and my co-facilitator left the room to be sick after less than 3 minutes! Proceed with care.

Conclusion

This paper has outlined some of the embodied effects of trauma and what can be done about them. It's a huge subject so it has just scratched the surface but I hope it will inspire curiosity, learning and embodied practitioners applying their skills to healing and peace work. Perhaps hope is the best note to end on after considering such a thorny subject. So on that note, let me comment that the biblical warning that the sins of the father will be visited onto the son for seven generations, which I hold as a warning of the lingering effects of trauma, need no longer be true. We have the understanding and the methodology to change it: That's worth celebrating and worth acting upon.

Mark Walsh is Director of Integration Training Ltd, the Embodied Facilitator Course and Achilles Resilience Training. He is an aikido blackbelt, long term meditator and has trained in numerous embodied systems such as yoga, body therapy, forms of dance and other martial arts.

He has extensive training and facilitation experience, primarily around leadership and resilience/trauma with large and small organisations in the UK and abroad, including: Unilever (London/ Switzerland), The UK House of Lords, Virgin Atlantic, Harrow Primary Care Trust (NHS London), The Institute of Development Studies (University of Sussex, Brighton), Shell, Axa, The Natural History Museum (London), Emerging Capital Partners (US/ Africa), Liberty Global (international telecoms blue-chip) and the Army of Sierra Leone. He also spent three years organising projects, training and conferences for the international organisation Aiki Extensions Inc in areas of conflict. This included leadership training, stress management and conflict resolution work in the Middle East alongside the UN, in the slums of Brazil and with an HIV awareness charity in East Africa.

Resources

I have made a number of accessible Youtube videos on this topic:

Embodied peace building

http://youtu.be/Fn38e8_VIKU

What is Trauma –

https://www.youtube.com/watch?v=n8dN1c1DRak

The body and trauma

http://youtu.be/xfci3IkFJRc

http://youtu.be/V2GQ9KKgPy0

Signs and Symptoms of Trauma –

https://www.youtube.com/watch?v=tie1YHvx-mo

Psychological Trauma / PTSD Resilience -

https://www.youtube.com/watch?v=Hee5elYC8rw

PTSD Trauma and Relationships –

https://www.youtube.com/watch?v=Ag3pclaD5n4

E-books by Paul Linden such as Embodied Peacemaking and Winning is

Healing (about abuse recovery) are excellent –

http://www.being-in-movement.com/resources/books

Babbette Roschild has written several good books, David Berchelli (TRE) is now widely taught, Waking the Tiger and other books by Peter Levine are good and there are many good PTSD self-help books.

Ritual: Embodied Method for Systemic Transformation - Zia Ali

It is highly conceivable, from the research of archaeologists, that ritual has been embedded within the human experience since at least the Middle Palaeolithic Age (300,000 years ago). Philip Lieberman, a cognitive scientist at Brown University, has researched burial rites during that era and suggests they may 'signify a concern for the dead that transcends daily life.' [9] But the question of why human beings create ritual is a study of a lifetime in itself, and cannot be addressed in any depth here. What interests me is the relationship between ritual and the state and psychological landscape of the body, how ritual can be devised as a tool to transform conflict and violence, and that its capacity to do so lies within its very impact on the body. Nevertheless, before we can begin to even touch the surface of this relationship it is worth briefly asking, ' What is ritual?'

---

[9] Lieberman, Philip, 'Uniquely Human' (1991)

What is Ritual?

Professor Stephan Feuchtwang, of the London School of Economics, defines ritual at its 'simplest' as ' the repeated and standardized communicative action.'[10] While one of the leading thinkers in Ritual Studies, Catherine Bell, captured ritual as a 'bodily strategy that produces an incarnate means of knowing.' In the International Encyclopaedia of the Social Sciences, the entry on ritual by Edmund Leach defines it as any form of repeated action that is not only functional or technical but also aesthetic. Ritual is, then, the aesthetic aspect of repeated action, conveying meaning that is also an expression of power.

What is clear is that ritual involves and impacts the human body. Any form of repeated gesture, movement, prayer, song, word requires the participation and function of the human body. What differentiates ritual from ceremony is the feature of repetition. A wedding ceremony made in public is intended to be a singular experience. But

---

[10] Feuchtwang, Stephan, From 'Ritual and Memory', Chapter 19 of ' Memory: Histories, Theories and Debates' ed. Radstone, S and Schwarz, B (2010); Fordham University Press

the renewal of vows can become a ritual for the couple in whatever way they choose. So what is the driver and purpose of this repetition? For one thing, in the case of renewing vows for instance, it signifies great importance and commitment. A couple renewing their vows frequently do so in order to demonstrate emotional, spiritual and social pledges to one another, and to consciously enscribe into both their private and public lives a sense of meaning and purpose. Ritual is an intrinsic human behaviour that consciously or unconsciously inculcates meaning into living experience, living worlds. Meaning often arises from the interior landscape of a person's beliefs, perceptions and values.

Making Meaning in the Body

So, if ritual is indeed a powerful tool for the making of meaning in human life, and is an action of the body, it makes sense to consider the impact of ritual on the human body itself. If the body is expressing a particular meaning or belief on a daily basis, that is something powerful to take note of. A brief look at principal rituals of collective religious prayer provide immediate clues as to the value system and cosmology of behaviour within specific cultures or religions. In Western Christianity, during a key stage of the worship service (Mass), the congregation kneel down and respond with repeated phrases at the prompt of the Priest. The posture is, to my judgement, unsupportive to the body and is a mild self-affliction of discomfort. This is deliberate; it is to mark and demonstrate the pain and suffering that Jesus Christ experienced before and during crucifixion. Yet shortly afterwards the same congregation stand up and receive the Eucharist (a portion of bread and a sip of wine). This demonstrates the belief of Jesus Christ's resurrection and the renewal of life after suffering and death. Observe too the various embodied rituals within Buddhism and chart the meaning-making process as expressed through the body. In Islam, prayers are frequently said in the position of kneeling and bowing upon the ground or a prayer mat. It is an embodiment of surrender, a submission to a power far greater. Many practices of yoga repeat asanas (body postures) in order to create a deeper harmony and integration of the human mind, body and spirit. It is both an embodied art of ritual and is designed to cultivate peace and awareness within this human lifetime. Repeated embodiment conditions the body not just physically but also instinctively to respond and act in certain ways to the situations of life.

The key of all this is the emotional content of the ritual. What effect does word or movement have on the person(s)? Does it provide relief, inspiration, fear, shame, pain, sadness? The state of the body can be dramatically impacted by ritual, because of its power of repetition. If the ritual is made publically, the feature of witnessing/witnesses adds another dimension to the experience. Being witnessed by another is to have one's own body witnessed. The meaning that the ritual creates, through the action itself or through its place within a wider belief-system or cosmology, in some way becomes a meaning for the person's body. Meaning is a fundamental shaper in human identity. It shapes behaviour and perception. At this point, having set the context, albeit loosely, I would like to focus on a theoretical synthesis I have been investigating in my doctoral research.

For some years I have been convinced that ritual and the performing arts were among the most transformative mediums within cultural life. During every effective conflict intervention I have engaged in – and this is across different countries including warzones like Afghanistan – the breakthroughs happened when the following occurred: people expressed how they really felt and what was most important to them, people shared a story that was either judged to be unspeakable or which simply felt unbearable even to remember let alone share, and perhaps most crucially to symbolically enact or honour a transition from one previous state or relationship to a new one. I gradually came to see these occurrences as being expressions of ritual and performance art. Consciously using mediums like drama and storytelling to represent fractious and emotionally charged realities of conflict quickly became an applied practice that I could adapt to widely different cultural contexts and the rituals came naturally, from the participants themselves. A constant element in this was a form of 'honouring' an experience in spite of its pain and horror, and the process of witnessing others and being witnessed in this moment of honouring. In each ritual, the symbolic reconfiguration of a new social constellation was expressed in a bodily enunciation, be it an embrace, a bow, a planting of flowers, a washing of hands, a handshake, a spoken prayer, a song or a physical gesture of renunciation. In two of the interventions I've been involved in, a systemic change resulted from the process. This led me to investigate systems theory, and it was during this research phase that I discovered two systemic models that seemed to correlate and complement one another.

The first of these models is DST (Dynamical Systems Theory), which is currently being applied to examining intractable conflict by Columbia University's Center for Cooperation and Conflict Resolution. The second is DMR Theory (Divergent Modes of Religiosity).

The theory of DMR proposes that religious organisations tend to cluster around two socio-political 'attractor positions': the one large-scale and hierarchical (Doctrinal mode) and the other highly cohesive but also localised or regionally fragmented (Imagistic mode). Research scholars at Oxford University, with funding from the ESRC (Economic and Social Research Council) have been applying DMR theory to understanding the formation for armed militia groups worldwide. The research investigates the rituals of these different groups, and how the rituals promote social cohesion while at the same time create distrust of groups with different ritual traditions. DMR theory, thus applied, synthesises with Dynamical Systems Theory, particular under its current applicability to identifying routes of interrupted intractable conflict.

The fundamental component in understanding DST is to look at the 'attractor paradigm'. An attractor is a subset of potential states of patterns of change to which a system converges over time. An attractor 'attracts' the system's behaviour, so that even very different starting states tend to evolve toward the subset of states defining the attractor. In other words, the attractor infiltrates and infuses the system. Once at its attractor, the system is resistant to external influences that would otherwise move the system to a different state or pattern of changes. This dynamic property helps us to understand why malignant social relations tend to be persistent over time and resistant to most interventions. However, the greatest potential for a sudden eruption of violence exists where there is a challenge to the validity of a party's attractor. So conversely, a violent system- such as an intractable war/conflict – can be interrupted if the attractor's validity is challenged.

It's my judgement that the Northern Ireland Peace Process achieved a breakthrough during the 90's because the depth of loss felt by people from all sides of the conflict weighed down so heavily that the previous political ideology driving the violence was no longer the 'attractor' it was once was. Instead, the 'attractor' was replaced by a desperate desire for the killing to end. The 'Yes' Campaign for people in both Northern Ireland and the Republic of Ireland to vote in a referendum for a devolved system of government perhaps signified a different 'attractor' undermining the validity of the previous one.

Conflict attractors are states or patterns that unfold overtime in situations of conflict which resist change or which resume after changes have been initiated. For instance when people face situations of conflict over a period of time they display certain tendencies to think, feel and react in particular ways. These tendencies can be strong, ones that overwhelmingly 'attract' the thoughts, feelings and behaviours involved in conflict, or weak tendencies representing a passing urge to react in a particular manner. Returning then to the DMR theory, ritual has the capacity to activate 'attractor' positions, a cosmological doctrine that provides a system of belief within which both individual and collective life has meaning, and a localised metaphorical or imagistic experience that creates a felt, embodied experience with social and material expressions of that larger abstract doctrine. On both individual and collective levels, it is possible to identify and track the attractors of conflict and violence, beginning with our own interior lives, the life of emotion, sensation, the body and mind. Trauma sufferers often experience heightened emotional charge within their bodies, sometimes the 'fight or flight' response, or the immobility response, anxiety, dissociation, nausea. What is happening in traumatic relapse is that the system of the body has been overridden by the replaying of the trauma, and it is the origin of the trauma i.e the traumatic experience/event itself, which acts as the 'attractor' within the dynamical system of the human body. So the validity of that attractor must be challenged and ultimately replaced.

The anthropologist Arnold van Gennep in his ground-breaking book 'The Rites of Passage', observed that ritual ceremonies that accompany the landmarks of human life differ only in detail from one culture to another but that they are in essence universal. He also coined the term 'liminal space', which refers to the space created by ritual which both has definite structure and form and is simultaneously without structure or form, and open to chaos. It is in this space that powerful transformation can, and does, happen. Catherine Bell in the seminal work of Ritual Studies called 'Ritual Theory, Ritual Practice' writes that, "Ritualization does not resolve a social contradiction. Rather it catches up into itself all the experienced and conventional conflicts and oppositions of social life, juxtaposing and homologizing them into a loose and provisional systematicity." [11]

Ritual, again in Bell's words, can "forge an experience of redemptive harmony" precisely because it is both participatory and performative. Whether it's an individual or a group ritual, it always involves an aesthetic and performative bodily communication.

This is why ritual is compelling. Like all performances it must be completed because it is an act of creating meaning, of telling a story, or communicating an idea usually so abstract that it must be somehow transmitted and translated through the performance medium. In contrast to physical and bodily habits picked up by most of us through mimicry, ritual contains a deliberately exaggerated embodiment in its intention to embed a teleology (or if you like, an unexpressed purpose or meaning) into the felt, embodied experience of human life. Like theatre, ritual is often witnessed by an audience. Like rehearsal, ritual refines and conditions an individual in the mode of performance and enunciatory communication. If the ceremony is done once, and is compelling enough for it to be repeated, then it becomes a ritual and has the capacity to transform the 'attractors' that might attract any

---

[11] Bell, Catherine, 'Ritual Theory, Ritual Practice', from the Chapter entitled ' The Ritual Body' pgs 105-6 (1992)

number of relationships and dynamics, be that conflict, violence, cohesion, creativity, collective grief or innovation. But what ritual does, in disengaging previous 'attractors' within the system of the human mind/body and engaging new 'attractors', is to draw a new map within the human body, and in doing so to create new embodied behaviours. In the fascinating book 'The Body of Myth' J.Nigro Sansonese explores myths as esoteric descriptions of what actually occurs within the human body, especially the human nervous system, during what he calls a 'trance'. This 'trance' bears striking resemblance to the kind of state people experience within the 'liminality' of the ritual space. Sansonese sees the human body as an atlas of mythic locale.

Ritual can perhaps be revisited as a timeless and perpetually proliferating human craft that can utilise its capacity to destroy as much as its capacity to regenerate. It is an evocatively and aesthetically embodied experience, both for participants and audience. It has the potential to dissolve dysfunction within social consciousness and transform social systems by transforming the bodily systems of both individuals and groups. Quite magically and – mythically – ritual is the pen that draws new maps within the atlas of the human body.

Zia Ali is a leadership and conflict resolution trainer, coach and doctoral researcher. He is based in North London and actively involved with mentoring charity A Band of Brothers, in co-facilitating 'rite of passage' mentoring programmes for young male offenders. Zia is also an Interfaith Minister, an artistic performer and creator of the PeaceFire Project, which delivers leadership and peace-building programmes using what Zia calls 'Performance Ritual'.

www.peacefireproject.org

Bibliography

Books:

Bell, Catherine, ' Ritual: Perspectives and Dimensions' (1997)

Bell, Catherine, 'Ritual Theory, Ritual Practice' (1992)

Levine, Peter, ' Waking the Tiger: Healing Trauma' (1997)

Scarry, Elaine, ' The Body in Pain' (1985)

Samonese Nigro. J, ' The Body of Myth: Mythology, Shamanic Trance and the Sacred Geography of the Body' (1994)

Radstone, Susannah and Schwarz, Bill, edited by, ' Memory: Histories, Theories, Debates' (2010)

Articles:

Whitehouse, Harvey, 'Ritual and Violence: Divergent Modes of Religiosity and Armed Struggle' (University of Oxford)

Liebovitch, Nowak and Bartoli, ' Intractable Conflict as a Dynamical System', International Center for the Study of Complexity and Conflict, Warsaw School of Social Psychology and Center for International Conflict Resolution, Columbia University

Innis. E, Robert, ' The Tacit Logic of Ritual Embodiments', from Social Analysis, Volume 48, Issue 2, Summer 2004

Journeying back to my body - Tom Kenward

My experience of embodiment work is that it is powerful stuff. My actions, thoughts and feelings have become imbued with a greater sense of clarity and conviction since embarking upon embodiment work. Those I work with somatically report similarly. I want to answer three questions in this article: what is the embodiment practice that works for me presently; what does that do for me and for those I work with; and finally, so what?! My intention is that the reader might recognise from this ways in which they too can, or already have, utilised embodiment work, feel encouraged in their onward journey, or become galvanized to take a first step into one of the myriad possibilities of embodiment work.

Pete Hamill refers to Mr Duffy in James Joyce's *Dubliners*, living *"a short distance from his body"* (2013, pg6). Hamill asks us to consider those we know who suffer this sort of distancing from their experience and sense of purpose. To be honest, it sums up how I experienced much of my life until recently and in my work I regularly encounter leaders who reach a similar realisation about themselves. I still retreat to my head on occasion, but working with my body has shown me and helped me accept who and what I am, and to grow into and beyond that with more confidence.

A few years back I encountered the leadership embodiment work of Wendy Palmer (Palmer and Crawford, 2013). I have great respect for and interest in many embodiment disciplines. I dwell on Wendy's work here only because it is what I have experienced the most of so far and therefore benefitted from and used with others. Assuming that many readers may not be familiar with this particular approach, I'll describe it a little. Firstly, it constitutes body and mind activities that challenge us to see clearly the habitual patterns of our mind and body when under pressure; the summary of mine being self-doubt, politeness and retreating into my thoughts. This work has helped me accept these parts of me, whilst not surrendering to them being all of who I am or what I can bring to the world. It has helped leaders who I have worked with too, to discover their own distinctive patterns, for example: overbearingly confident; fiercely outspoken; strong and persistent yet unable to see a different view or bigger picture; independent and reliable, yet exhausted. None of these patterns are better or worse, in fact our patterns are all dysfunctional, because they all damage our connection to other people and the wider world, which then reduces our capacity to act effectively and resourcefully. But there's better news in this work too. Firstly, it's easier to spot my patterns in the moment when I'm looking for body, not just mental, cues. When I am under pressure my tendency shows up in my body before I even notice in my mind: my head drops, my chest shrinks and, if I'm standing, my hips drop back. Secondly, if I catch this early, I have a better chance of halting the response that would otherwise send me deeper into my pattern, narrowing my perception and, with it, choices. In that moment of greater awareness, I have more clarity, confidence and compassion than my body had been gearing me up for moments earlier. And this is important for leaders I work with too – we can learn the latest theory and methods, but if we can't catch ourselves in the moments when we need to enact them, what use are they?

A question which then arises is: Even if we do catch ourselves, can we actually do something different? The work also offers us body-based techniques to intervene in our personality-based patterns, not to dismiss the value or presence of our personality, but to add to it with a particular version of that common embodiment term – centre. The words 'personality' and 'centre' both have particular meanings here. Personality is defined as the part of us we all possess that references to security – the need to be in control, to feel approval and safety. Centre on the other hand gives us more expansiveness, clarity, compassion and confidence, helping us to express ourselves more fully in the world. Having defined the words, we move to the body, deploying ways to align to and connect into this centre in ourselves physically. These days, I can find at least something close to this centre, by: uplifting posture up my back then softening down my front with in and out breaths respectively; extending my awareness of the space inside and outside my body; settling with gravity; and finally bringing to awareness core qualities. The method goes beyond the core exercises of seeing our patterns and finding our centre, but these foundations are very strong and I'll give an example shortly. [Editor's Note – Other similar methods for 'centring' were described in Volume One of EJ by Clare Myatt and Mark Walsh references similar techniques in his article here]

Wendy's outlook and experience helps greatly too, I believe. Namely, a respect and admiration of human potential, counterweighted by a hawk-like yet loving attention to the personality's patterns – like those I mention – that have the constant potential to separate us from the world and each other and stifle our potential. Also running deep through the work is Wendy's long experience of both Aikido and Tibetan mindfulness practice.

Seeking a more embodied existence started before finding this work though. Other experiences have contributed which I list here in case they help you acknowledge the breadth of ways in which you may be strengthening your mind-body relationship. Mine has been aided by school athletics, tennis and football, cranio-osteopathy, acupuncture, Alexander technique, Ayurvedic medicine, NLP, bioenergetic therapy, cycling, dance, drumming, and sex. This all brought me to a point a few years ago when I embarked upon the more conscious embodiment work I have outlined.

Moving to my second question, here's a concrete example of how embodiment work is bringing me into a richer way of being which I find helps me live more fully in myself and with those around me. It's about conflict and love. Last week I became entangled in a difficult conversation with my (wonderful) partner about a small but important perception of different views which mattered to us both. My first attempt still didn't go well: standing over the sink as I washed up breakfast dishes, the first words from my partner caused my gut to contract and I felt a thin line of heat and tension move up my torso to my head. I didn't take the moment needed to catch myself and fully centre, and I was identified with a sense of feeling wronged already, but I stayed engaged for a while thanks to reaching toward centre during the exchange. My body couldn't really get beyond the oppressive weight of resenting the original comment though, which meant I couldn't open to a fuller meaning of the message; eventually I just exploded into an angry shout and that was that! What did go better was the second attempt at the other end of the day. I took time (a minute or so) to centre as described previously and visualised a bubble around me, not as a shield but as a means to give me a little longer to process what my partner was saying. I was able to hear a key piece of what was being offered which I was previously too defended to hear, namely that I hadn't made a clear enough request in the first place about what I wanted. The practice of 'centred listening' (Palmer and Crawford, 2013, pg51) was essential here, as it allowed me to listen for the whole and not take the message so personally. I heard and accepted this as valid and was also able to stay in the conversation and become more responsible for my part in the mix up, then to voice cleanly yet gently my own views. I ended that conversation feeling that my and my partner's needs and views had been understood and met enough and something for each of us had been honoured and worked with, bringing us into connection so we could return there again with a little more confidence.

Until recently, such interactions have been more tiring and less productive than the above example. My fear of having to work with a view or need different from mine was too much for my personality to handle. I would receive the difference as a questioning of or even attack upon my ok-ness, in transactional analysis terms (Stewart and Joines, 2009). I might then retreat to simmer in self-righteousness or confusion before trying again. Eventually, I might reach a reasonably satisfactory resolution or compromise in a follow up conversation, though often still missing the real heat of the difference which lay dishonoured to some extent for me and/or the other. In contrast, the kindness, confidence and clarity I have found in centre has been a relief. I still get caught off balance sometimes, but finding centre brings me closer to a full contact in gestalt therapeutic terms (Houston, 2007) with the people and issues involved, giving me more courage and sensitivity in the conversation.

When leaders I work with try centred listening on for size, it is often an enlightening moment for them too. Some realise that 'being strong' might in fact require more openness to feedback and that they can receive this without feeling attacked or 'looking weak'. Others realise that they need to speak less, but that in centre they can be quieter without disappearing from others' awareness. Others still realise that they do need to be more direct in speaking their own voice, but that this doesn't have to be experienced as aggressive to the other or exhausting for them. The point is that, while there are hundreds of theories and methods for everything from assertiveness to visionary leadership to empowering and engaging people, only a few of these help much with supporting us to *be* more of what and who we already are. And through a fuller sense of being, the doing of whatever is needed becomes more impactful and we might then realise that we don't need any more theories or models.

This development has also changed my view of and appetite for conflict. I can now accept in practice my long held espoused view that conflict is an essential part of meeting and moving with people in our differences, rather than it being an ugly or painful obstacle. I don't go looking for fights and I still make mistakes, but I am now more present in such conversations. The way I make meaning of this change in my response relates to the definition of personality I gave previously. With the help of centre, I can now spot when the insecurities of my personality distort my perception and seek more security. In one way or another, for all of us, personality narrows perception and separates us from those around us. From that awareness I can take the few seconds I need to breathe, align my body in the space around me and settle my personality response through relaxing the muscle tension that will have accompanied the drawing in of my personality's defences. Then I can respond with a clearer focus, confidence and love. Again, my experiences of working with leaders is that they become more courageous in working with and through conflict rather than seeing conflict as a battle to the death with one winner. This may sound utopian in the cut and thrust of business, but my experience has been that the sense of possibilities and respect that people find when they connect with centre is extremely useful even in previously stuck interpersonal dynamics. I said that this example was about conflict and love. The sense of safety and compassion we can find in accessing centre is essential if we are to step in and fully meet the heat of others' difference in a leadership setting. This doesn't mean that everyone will then agree, but it does mean that we give ourselves a much better chance of understanding the difference and then, with greater respect and trust, move forward with more commitment.

Beyond conflict, the utility of centre extends to other situations where I experience pressure because, basically, all are variations of my personality running for security, and centre can always help out. For example, returning to the office this week after several days out has meant many competing demands on my time. I kept my feet flat on the floor and my chair high, so that my pelvis stayed tipped forward and my spine naturally extended upwards, I kept breathing, paying particular attention to a long out breath. This allowed me to prioritise before narrowing in on tasks, then focus on one thing at a time. These are the body and brain processes I attend to presently – if I can notice my tendency to 'get hooked' straight away, I can then reposition myself physically which then immediately gives me a more expansive set of choices mentally and emotionally.

As I address my own detachment between mind and body, I see how crucial this issue may be for others. I meet many leaders on their own journeys of development, who at some point in earlier life developed some degree of coping mechanism by retreating to their thoughts. But they are now finding a way back from that narrow state of being, to discover they have far more to offer. I see our damaging acts towards ourselves, each other and the world as stemming from a lack of one or more of love, confidence or vision and I now realise these can only be accessed fully when we are reasonably well integrated in mind and body.

I am now accustomed to the initial skepticism from some of those I introduce to this work, to paraphrase: "so is that it then, I just sit, stand and breath differently then I'll lead better?". A fair challenge perhaps, but within it lurk two underestimates: how greatly these basic body habits define what and who we are and, secondly, how difficult it can be to adjust these habits with consistency and effectiveness when we most need to. But that's a whole other article. Those moments of greatest need could be anything, from when my four year old son refuses to go to bed, to when I am supporting an unsettled leader to see that, by finding greater courage, they can make a better decision. Having undertaken many development processes over decades, today it is embodiment work which makes the biggest difference to me being able to intervene consciously and effectively in my own thoughts and actions during those moments. I delight in this, and in seeing others finding value in their various embodied journeys. I don't claim to have reached this point, but the words of Trungpa Rinpoche resonate strongly with my sense of the power of this work:

When you are fully gentle, without arrogance and without aggression, you see the brilliance of the universe. (1984, p130)

That's a good aspiration to reach for, I feel.

Tom Kenward works as a senior consultant at the Roffey Park Institute. He runs the *MSc in People and Organisation Development* and an Open Programme, *Leading with Presence*. He also designs and delivers bespoke programmes to develop leaders and organisational development practitioners, using somatic methods as part of these. He does his best to practice (and practise) what he preaches with lightness, at work and also with his partner Charlotte and two young children Toby and Rose, sometimes remembering to call forth in the more testing moments the Buddhist mantra of "begin again".

On LinkedIn: http://linkd.in/1DYoD0E

Bibliography

Cuddy, A.J.C., Kohut, M. and Neffinger, J. 2013. Connect, then Lead. Harvard Business Review. July/August, 91 (7/8) 54-61.

Hamill, P. 2013. Embodied Leadership – The somatic approach to developing your leadership. Kogan Page, UK.

Houston, G. 2007. The now red book of Gestalt. Published by Gaie Houston, London.

Palmer, W. and Crawford, J. 2013. Leadership Embodiment – How the way we sit and stand can change the way we think and speak. CreateSpace, California.

Stewart, I. and Joines, V. 2009. TA Today – A new introduction to Transactional Analysis. Lifespace Publishing and Chapel Hill.

Trungpa, C. 1984. Shambhala – The Sacred Path of the Warrior. Shambhala Publications, Boston.

www.embodimentjournal.com

Printed in Dunstable, United Kingdom